No more debt

Allen Carr

No more debt

ARCTURUS

To Tim Glynne-Jones and Nigel Matheson – with
thanks for their invaluable and inspired work in
helping to apply Easyway to new areas of addiction

ARCTURUS

This edition published in 2018 by Arcturus Publishing Limited
26/27 Bickels Yard, 151–153 Bermondsey Street,
London SE1 3HA, UK

Copyright © 2018 Allen Carr's Easyway (International) Limited

ISBN: 978-1-78404-540-1
AD004272UK

Printed in the UK

ABOUT ALLEN CARR

Allen Carr was a chain-smoker for over 30 years. In 1983, after countless failed attempts to quit, he went from 100 cigarettes a day to zero without suffering withdrawal pangs, without using willpower, and without putting on weight. He realized that he had discovered what the world had been waiting for – the easy way to stop smoking – and embarked on a mission to help cure the world's smokers.

As a result of the phenomenal success of his method, he gained an international reputation as the world's leading expert on stopping smoking and his network of clinics now spans the globe. His first book, *Allen Carr's Easy Way to Stop Smoking*, has sold over 12 million copies, remains a global best-seller, and has been published in more than 40 different languages. Hundreds of thousands of smokers have successfully quit at Allen Carr's Easyway Clinics where, with a success rate of over 90%, he guarantees you'll find it easy to stop or your money back.

Allen Carr's Easyway method has been successfully applied to a host of issues including weight control, alcohol and other addictions, debt, gambling, and fears. A list of Allen Carr clinics appears at the back of this book. Should you require any assistance or if you have any questions, please do not hesitate to contact your nearest clinic. For more information about Allen Carr's Easyway, please visit

www.allencarr.com

INTRODUCTION

Having a debt problem is not the same
as having debts. Millions of people have
huge debts in the form of a mortgage, yet
they're not miserable, stressed or scared.
They simply regard their debt as a business
transaction that stretches over a long period.
'Problem debt' is very different. It causes
terrible anxiety and misery and is often
suffered in secret, such is society's attitude
to people in financial difficulty. Tragically,
problem debt affects millions of people
around the world.

There are some classic signs of problem debt:

You start missing payments, e.g. on a credit card

You avoid opening bills

You avoid friends and family members who have lent you money

You stop spending money on genuine pleasures like recreation and entertainment

You lie about your financial situation

These are all proof that your debts are controlling you. When you find yourself in this situation, escape can seem impossible. The good news is that escape is actually easy, provided you follow the correct method.

It's a matter of understanding the trap you're in and following a simple set of instructions to get out.

Allen Carr's Easyway method has helped thousands of people to quit smoking, alcohol and other drugs, as well as to stop gambling, overeating and being trapped in debt. It works by unravelling the misconceptions that make you believe that you get some benefit from the very thing that's harming you.

This book applies the same method to unravel the misconceptions that make you believe you get some pleasure or crutch from spending money you don't have on things you don't need.

Unlike other methods, it does not require willpower. All you have to do is read the book in its entirety, follow all the instructions and you cannot fail to cure your debt problem.

The solution is in your hands!

IS DEBT A PROBLEM?

Millions of people are in debt. They take out loans to buy houses, cars, holidays, clothes. In some cases, they have no intention of paying them off for years and yet this is not a cause of stress for them.

But for others, debt becomes a real problem. I can only assume that includes you.

It feels like a trap, a prison from which there is no escape. Whichever way you turn, you just seem to go deeper into debt.

WHY WE FIND IT SO HARD TO ESCAPE

Finding your own way out of the debt trap is virtually impossible. Why? Because most people assume that the only way to escape is through sheer willpower. But the willpower method tackles your problem in reverse – like a mirror that shows everything upside down. The more you try to get out, the deeper in debt you will go.

In order to escape, you need to follow a method that tackles the source of your problem, not the symptoms.

QUITTING THE EASY WAY

Getting out of debt is easy if you approach it in the right way. All you need to do is unravel the illusions that led you into debt in the first place.

All debt is caused by one thing and one thing alone: spending money you do not have. You may have many reasons for doing this, but the simple fact is that the only way you are going to get out of debt is to stop spending money you don't have.

With Allen Carr's Easyway, you will find that easy to achieve. All you need to do is follow all the instructions.

CURING THE BIGGEST FEAR IN THE WORLD

This method was originally devised to cure smoking, the world's number one addiction. It became a global phenomenon, helping millions of smokers to quit easily and permanently by removing the misconceptions that bring about the fear that causes nicotine addiction.

Perhaps you can't see a connection between smoking and overspending and don't regard your problem as addiction. Many people who overspend think it's just a habit they can't shake because they lack the willpower. As long as they believe this, they remain in the debt trap.

WHAT'S ALL THIS ABOUT ADDICTION?

Addiction does not only apply to drugs such as nicotine, alcohol and heroin. Addiction can also be behavioural, such as gambling and overeating. Now add to that overspending.

As with all addictions, overspending is a man-made condition, which starts small, seemingly under control, but soon grows to the point where it takes you over and threatens to destroy your life.

In their confusion, all addicts seek relief from their torment in the very thing that's tormenting them.

THE ILLUSION OF PLEASURE

With all addictions, it's the illusion that the substance or behaviour provides a genuine pleasure or crutch that keeps you trapped. For example, smokers believe that cigarettes help them relax. In fact, they do the complete opposite. The illusion of relaxation is caused by the partial and temporary relief of the slightly uncomfortable physical feeling of withdrawal, coupled with the anxiety brought about by massive brainwashing from an early age. But because they perceive this temporary relief as pleasure, smokers are afraid to quit because they think they will lose something valuable from their lives.

WHY SMOKERS SMOKE

As the nicotine leaves the body, smokers start to feel edgy and anxious. Because they're under the illusion that cigarettes relax them, they smoke another cigarette. This introduces more nicotine into the body, temporarily and partially relieving the symptoms of discomfort, but guaranteeing that those feelings will return when the next dose leaves the smoker's body. It is this cycle that convinces the smoker that cigarettes relax them.

Non-smokers do not have this problem.

Smokers smoke in order to feel like non-smokers!

WHY DEBTORS KEEP SPENDING

A similar cycle takes place when you're addicted to spending. The chemicals in the brain are triggered by overspending in very much the same way that they are triggered by nicotine and other drugs, creating a reaction that mimics the effect of genuine pleasures. Unlike genuine pleasures, it doesn't last and we are left with an irritable, insecure feeling. Instead of realizing that overspending is the cause of this unpleasant feeling, we think the very opposite, so we do it again. And so the cycle is repeated.

The only way to break the cycle is to stop overspending.

YOU ARE NOT ALONE

The world is full of people suffering the agony of debt and most of them are suffering in silence. Debt is a taboo that causes a sense of shame and failure. But it is nothing to be ashamed about, nor is it a failure in you. The reason so many people, rich, poor, high paid and low paid, suffer debt problems is because debt involves an addiction that, like all addictions, traps addicts in a downward spiral from which they don't know how to escape.

Yet the harmful effects of debt prey on all sufferers individually. The fact that millions of others are experiencing the same suffering does not lessen its impact on you.

FORGET YOUR FAILURES

Perhaps you've attempted to get out of
debt in the past and found you couldn't.
No matter how hard you tried, you
felt you lacked the willpower. Trying
and failing reinforces the illusion that
getting out of the debt trap is hard. It
doesn't cross your mind that you've been
following a method that doesn't work.
Now you spend money you don't have,
even when you don't want to, and you're
powerless to stop.

In fact, you're not powerless and you don't
lack willpower.

If you've made failed attempts to control
your spending in the past it's simply
because you were following the wrong
method.

FREEDOM STARTS HERE

This book will give you all the help you need to unravel the illusions that have kept you trapped in debt. You now hold the key to your own prison. Remember, whatever methods you may have tried have not worked, so dismiss all the misinformation you've been fed up until now and free your mind to follow a method that has already enabled millions of people to escape from slavery.

The method makes escape easy. All you need to do is follow all the instructions.

THE MOST IMPORTANT INSTRUCTION

First instruction: FOLLOW ALL THE INSTRUCTIONS.

This may sound like a joke but I assure you it isn't. Allen Carr's Easyway works like the combination of a safe. If I give you the combination and you follow it in order and in its entirety, the safe will open easily. But miss out any of the numbers, or use them in the wrong order, and the safe will remain firmly locked.

The first instruction is the most important. Follow this one and you cannot fail.

THE GREAT TABOO

Why do we even think that spending money will make us happy? Because that is what we are told to believe from an early age.

From the moment we are old enough to understand the exchange of money for goods, we are brainwashed to believe two myths:

that spending leads to happiness

that money equals success

We all want success and happiness but you won't find it by living beyond your means. That's a recipe for failure and misery.

MIXED MESSAGES

'Take care of the pennies and the pounds
will take care of themselves.'

'In for a penny, in for a pound.'

The messages we get about money drive us
to opposite extremes. So which should you
be: a miser or a spendthrift?

The fact is that both sorts of people are
labouring under the same misconception:
that money is of paramount importance, a
sure sign of success, and so they allow it to
dominate their lives.

THE SECOND INSTRUCTION

This method will enable you to regain control of your finances without using willpower or feeling any sense of deprivation or sacrifice. You will be able to buy everything you need and lead a rich and fulfilling life, while clearing your debts and rebuilding your relationships, making you happier than you can imagine.

This is my claim, but whether you believe it or not has no bearing at this stage. A combination lock opens regardless of whether the person putting in the numbers believes it will.

Second instruction: KEEP AN OPEN MIND.

What have you got to lose?

QUESTION EVERYTHING YOU KNOW

Keeping an open mind is vital if you want to see the truth. For example, what do you see below? One square table and one rectangular one, right?

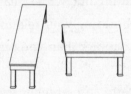

You've accepted that it's one square table and one rectangular one because that's what it looks like and I've suggested that it is. Now if I were to tell you that the dimensions of each table are exactly the same, would you believe me?

I assure you they are. Take a ruler and measure them. Being open-minded means questioning everything, even when you are convinced that you know the answer.

WHY WE GET INTO DEBT

The delusion that you can buy happiness drives you to spend more than you have, which in reality leads to misery. The more you try to find happiness by overspending, the deeper into debt you plunge and the more miserable you become.

If you spend more than you have, you'll get into debt. Whether you do it to the tune of £50 or £50,000, the principle is the same. Whether you earn a meagre wage or you're a millionaire, if you spend more than you have and cannot pay it off, the debt is only going to do one thing: grow.

THE F WORD

Some people will do virtually anything in their power to keep the truth about their debts from others. Worse, they will also deny the truth to themselves. That's because accepting that we have a debt problem can make us feel a failure.

Being in debt doesn't mean you are a failure.

All that's happened is you have been trapped, along with millions of other people. The good news is that you can walk out of that trap any time you choose.

HAPPINESS

The true measure of success is happiness.
Anyone can attain happiness, regardless
of their financial situation. Happiness has
nothing to do with money.

The aim of this book is to make you happy.
Right now, debt is making you miserable
and you are anxious that getting out of
debt will make life harder still. I assure
you this is not the case. The process is
absolutely painless and the good times
start the moment you stop incurring new
debts. You have nothing to lose and only
marvellous gains to look forward to.

A TUG-OF-WAR

The overspending addict suffers a constant tug-of-war. You know it's causing you harm and misery and threatening to destroy your life, yet you feel compelled to go on doing it. You know that the only sensible thing to do is quit, yet you suspect that quitting will be more painful than carrying on because you still believe that spending gives you some kind of pleasure or crutch.

You feel the only thing that can save you is a miracle.

MAKING IT EASY

The tug-of-war is caused by conflicting information. On one side is the knowledge that your debts are ruining your life; on the other is the false belief that spending gives you some form of pleasure or crutch and that if you stop spending you'll be miserable.

As soon as you understand and believe that spending is an addiction that provides no genuine pleasure or crutch, and that once you are free you won't feel miserable or deprived, you win the tug-of-war. With no illusions to pull against, victory is easy.

THE THIRD INSTRUCTION

Regardless of whether you believe what I've said so far, it's important that you continue to follow the instructions. I've asked you to keep an open mind: that means accepting that what I say could be true, even if you suspect it to be false. As you continue to read, give yourself time to merely consider the possibility that what I say is correct. What do you have to lose? If I am wrong, you are no worse off than when you started. If I am right, you will become free from your debt worries forever.

So banish all feelings of doom and gloom from your mind and keep following the instructions.

Third instruction: START OFF IN A HAPPY FRAME OF MIND RATHER THAN WITH A FEELING OF DOOM AND GLOOM.

SPENDING AND OTHER ADDICTIONS

All addicts are caught in an ingenious trap that leads them to believe that salvation lies in the very thing that's causing the misery. They only crave what they see as their little crutch when they can't have it; when they have it, they wish they didn't have it.

If you spend because you think it will give you some sort of high, you are chasing an illusion. The truth is it will do the exact opposite; it will make you miserable.

That's how addiction works, but when you're in the trap you don't see things as they really are.

JUNK SPENDING

We all need to spend money to a certain extent. The best things in life may well be free, but not everything is. The basic essentials – food, warmth and shelter – cost money. However, we don't just spend money on these essentials. We also spend on a whole host of other things, many of which are not only useless from a practical point of view but also give us no genuine pleasure whatsoever.

This is what I call junk spending. It is the spending equivalent of junk food.

THE MYTH OF CONTROL

When you spend money you don't have, it can make you forget your money worries temporarily. It gives you a feeling of control, which feels like a great relief from the constant anxiety of having a debt problem. When you spend in this way, it briefly tricks you into feeling like someone who has no financial problems.

But all it's doing is sending you deeper into debt; and as your debts get worse you start to sense that you're not really in control. It's just an illusion. It's the feeling of losing control that causes the anxiety.

I'M NOT A SHOPAHOLIC!

Perhaps you think this book is aimed at people who can't resist the temptation to go shopping. That might seem trivial compared to the scale of your debt. You might have lost a fortune in a failed business venture or as a result of some other unhappy event.

The fact is, all debt is caused by the same thing: spending money you don't have. If you then fail to address your debt and borrow more money in order to carry on, you fall into the same trap.

FILLING A VOID

As we grow up we suffer a series of disillusionments that create a void in our lives. The comfort we receive as infants is replaced by being pushed out into the world and fear and insecurity rush in to fill the vacuum. Instinctively we look for support, for a little boost now and then. We look to our role models and copy the things they appear to do for comfort and relaxation: drink, smoke, shop.

Trouble is, these things don't fill the void; they make it worse.

THE FLAW IN THE MACHINE

The thing that sets man above all other species is intelligence. In addition to the survival instincts that we share with other animals, we have the intellectual capacity to pass on information.

We can also pass on misinformation.

Much of this misinformation goes against our instincts. That's why, despite sensing instinctively that spending money we don't have might be harming us, we tell ourselves that it's OK to carry on. We trust the brainwashing over our instincts.

This is the flaw in the incredible human machine.

DISTINGUISHING FACT FROM ILLUSIONS

How can you be sure that what I am telling you is true and everything else is an illusion? What if the opposite is the case?

Turn back to the optical illusion on page 24. If you followed my suggestion and measured the two tables, you will now know without a shadow of a doubt that they share the same dimensions. And knowing that, you can never again be fooled into thinking they are different.

That's what happens when you see through an illusion. With junk spending, once you can see that it does absolutely nothing for you, you will never again be led to believe that it does.

HOW WE GET TRAPPED

The debt trap is similar to a pitcher plant, which lures flies into its chamber with the sweet smell of nectar. The fly lands on the rim and begins to drink. The nectar tastes good; it seems like the best thing in the world. But it is the very thing that is luring the fly to its death. By the time the fly realizes the seriousness of the situation it's too late. The pitcher plant claims another victim.

With the debt trap, you begin with small debts, then take on bigger debts in an attempt to regain control, all the time slipping further and further in.

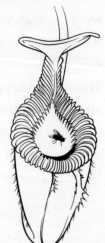

NATURE'S WARNING LIGHT

Imagine you're driving a car and the oil light comes on. What do you do? Remove the bulb from the warning indicator? Or pull over and top up the oil? Both actions will stop the oil light from flashing; only one will prevent the engine from seizing up.

Discomfort is nature's way of telling us we have a problem that needs to be dealt with. If we take an anaesthetic we may remove the pain temporarily, but the problem does not go away. In fact, it gets worse.

This is what we do when we spend in an attempt to relieve our misery.

IGNORING THE SIGNS

When the fly senses that it's in danger, does it stop drinking and fly away? No, it continues to drink until it is consumed by the pitcher plant.

When a problem debtor realizes he has a debt problem, does he stop spending? No, he tries to blot out the miserable truth by spending more.

Gamblers, smokers, heroin addicts... all addicts behave in the same way. They address the symptoms, not the cure.

The cunning nature of the trap means they seek relief in the very thing that is causing the problem.

GENUINE PLEASURES

If the brain can be deceived into believing that spending makes us happy, does it matter that it isn't true?

Yes it does, because the reality is that it's doing the complete opposite. It is forcing you deeper and deeper into debt and making you more and more anxious and miserable.

You can tell that junk spending is not a genuine pleasure because it doesn't leave you feeling happy and satisfied when it stops. Genuine pleasures do.

Take some time to examine the pleasures you think you get from spending in more detail and ask yourself, 'Are these genuine pleasures? Do they leave me with a lasting feeling of happiness?'

SELLING MISINFORMATION

The world is full of people with a vested interest in selling you misinformation.

Salespeople have many strategies for hooking their prey. But if they have to go to such lengths to manoeuvre us into a position where we feel obliged to buy, doesn't that suggest that we don't really want what they're selling?

Advertisers and salespeople will argue that they are merely trying to persuade you to buy one brand over another, but actually they spend most of their time persuading people to buy products they don't need.

BUY ONE GET ONE FREE

A popular sales strategy for some people is to create the impression that they're not desperate for your money. The idea of getting two things you need for the price of one is attractive. But BOGOFs (Buy One Get One Free) are designed to make you buy things you didn't even want one of. By creating the illusion of good value, they let you convince yourself of a reason to buy. But when you entered the shop, you had no need or desire to buy.

You're not saving money, you're spending more than you intended to.

GIVE 'EM ENOUGH ROPE

There are many other sales traps that you need to see through, all of which are designed to entice you into buying something against your instincts.

Interest free credit

0% finance

Buy now, pay later

Interest free credit gives buyers the rope to hang themselves. Money-lenders make their profit from debt. Interest-free credit is their bait.

CREDIT CARDS

A credit card can take on an almost mystical power. It is seen as the key to all sorts of pleasures, an all-knowing fixer that opens doors, removes obstacles, solves problems and saves embarrassment. Of equal importance to what it can do for you is what it seems to say about you. A credit card is seen as a status symbol, something that can earn you respect.

This is all part of an elaborate con to lure you into debt. Let's be quite clear about this: you don't own your credit card – it owns you!

CAVEAT EMPTOR

If you want further proof that Big Retail
relies on illusions, look no further than
the salesperson's motto: caveat emptor
– let the buyer beware! This is the legal
principle that a buyer makes a purchase at
his or her own risk.

Would there be a need for such a principle
if sellers were open and honest about all
aspects of their products, good and bad?
But any salesperson will tell you that they
would sell a good deal less. Why? Because
customers would see the products for what
they really are and realize that they neither
need nor want them.

The illusion would be stripped away.

BUYING IS NOT LOVING

A little boy is alone in his room. He wants
his dad to play with him, but dad is busy.
Dad feels for his son and wants him to
be happy, so at some point he buys him
a toy. At first the boy is delighted but
after a while the toy bores him. What he
really wants is companionship and love.
He throws the toy against the wall and
smashes it. Dad hears the noise and comes
running. He's angry. The little boy cries.
Dad feels awkward and wants to cheer him
up. He goes out and buys another toy…

We can all see the flaw in this scenario.
Why can't we see it in our own lives?

MONSTERS

With addiction, I call the uncomfortable
feeling of withdrawal the Little Monster.
The Little Monster is created when you
start spending for pleasure or a crutch and
continues to grow the more you spend. It
is an empty, dissatisfied, insecure feeling –
the Little Monster crying out to be fed.

The cries of the Little Monster awake
the Big Monster. This is the monster in
your head that tells you the only way to
satisfy the Little Monster is to spend. The
Big Monster is created by brainwashing.
Destroy the Big Monster and the Little
Monster quickly goes the same way.

AN INEVITABLE DECLINE

Every time the father buys his son a present to console him, the present has to be bigger and better than the last one. The same applies when we spend money for our own sense of pleasure or a crutch.

This is due to tolerance, our natural protective mechanism that builds a layer against things that are bad for us. As the layer builds, you have to spend more and more to get any sense of relief at all. Each withdrawal sends you crashing down to a new low.

This is how addiction drags us down. The only way to halt the decline is to stop feeding the Little Monster.

TIME TO SEE THE REALITY

The idea that money buys happiness is a myth. You can see it plainly in the case of the spoilt child, now you need to see it in your own case.

The reality of spending money you haven't got is far from happy. It leads to:

Being a slave to debt

Fear

Evasiveness

Stress

Loss of trust and respect

Breakdown of relationships

Legal problems

Misery

Follow your instincts. If you feel instinctively that you can't afford something, it's usually a sign that you don't really need or want it.

TIGHT SHOES

It's important to understand the exchange between the temporary relief you get from feeding the Little Monster and the ever-increasing misery that results.

It's like walking around in tight shoes all day, just to get the relief of taking them off. Is that your idea of a genuine pleasure? What do you think would happen to your feet over time?

This is what all addicts effectively do, but only because they don't understand the trap they're in.

NEVER TOO LATE TO ESCAPE

Like the fly in the pitcher plant, the more you spend to feed the Little Monster, the further you slide into the trap.

Unlike the fly, you have the power to escape.

The fly keeps drinking the nectar because it can't see that the nectar is what's leading it to its doom. But you're not standing on a slippery slope. There is no physical force compelling you to spend. The trap is entirely in your mind. As soon as you recognize and understand that junk spending is not a pleasure or a crutch but is what's leading you to your doom, you can escape whenever you want.

UNRAVELLING THE MYTHS

The ingenuity of the trap is that it makes you your own jailer. But this is also its fundamental flaw – you can escape any time you choose. Right now there are just two things stopping you from making that choice:

1. The myth that spending gives you pleasure and/or a crutch.

2. The myth that escape will be hard and may be impossible.

Both myths contribute to the single force that keeps all addicts hooked:

FEAR.

THE FEAR OF FAILURE

Fear of failure is another of nature's great driving forces. It is what makes the great dancer perfect her steps, the great athlete train extra hard.

Fear of failure drives us on to achieve great things.

If you have tried to get out of debt in the past, you will know what failure feels like. It is not a pleasant experience. But if you allow the fear of failure to prevent you from even trying, then you guarantee that you will fail.

You cannot avoid failure if you don't try.

THE FEAR OF SUCCESS

Have you ever heard of anyone fearing success? It's actually what keeps all addicts in the trap.

The fear of being deprived of your pleasure or crutch, the fear that you've got to go through a period of deprivation and frustration to get free and the fear that maybe you'll never be completely free from the misery of debt or the perception of restricted spending.

The fear of success comes from not understanding what success really looks like.

HABIT OR ADDICTION?

Addicts make excuses for their behaviour. A common one is that it's just a habit they can't seem to shake. This creates the impression that they are in control and could stop any time they set their mind to it. Addicts have to convince themselves of this because the alternative is too horrible to face: that they are helpless slaves.

But when they do set their mind to stopping, they find they can't. They assume they lack the willpower.

Recognize that it's not a question of willpower but addiction and you can quickly escape from the trap.

THE PERSONALITY DELUSION

Addicts tend to see themselves as part of a special breed. They feel a great kinship with one another and seek comfort in each other's company. They regard those who are not one of them as alien and threatening and fear that quitting would put them on the outside with those people.

Thanks to the influence of role models, junk spenders like to see themselves as carefree, fun-loving types who aren't bothered by mundane matters like living within their means. They fear that imposing stricter controls on their spending will make life hard and boring.

But the misery of debt is already hard and boring.

WILLPOWER – THE HARD OPTION

The simplest of tasks becomes difficult
if you go about it the wrong way. Think
about opening a door. You push on the
handle and it swings open with the
minimum of effort. But have you ever
tried pushing on the wrong side where
the hinges are? You meet with instant
resistance. The door might budge a tiny
bit, but it won't swing open. It requires a
huge amount of effort and determination.
Push on the correct side and the door
opens without you even having to think
about it.

HOW WILLPOWER KEEPS YOU HOOKED

With the willpower method, you focus on all the reasons for stopping and hope you can hold out long enough for the desire to spend to eventually disappear.

The problem is that you still perceive spending as a pleasure or crutch and, therefore, you feel you've made a sacrifice. This feeling of deprivation makes you miserable, which in turn makes you want to cheer yourself up by doing the one thing you've vowed not to do – junk spend.

Allen Carr's Easyway removes the need for willpower by removing the illusion that you're making a sacrifice.

HOW WEAK-WILLED ARE YOU?

Ask yourself whether you're weak-willed
in other ways. Perhaps you're a smoker or
you eat or drink too much, and you regard
these conditions as further evidence of a
weak will. There's a connection between
all addictions, but the connection isn't that
they're signs of a lack of willpower. On the
contrary, they're more likely evidence of a
strong will.

It takes a stubborn will to keep doing
something in the face of so many reasons
to stop. Think of the lengths you've gone
to in order to feed your addiction. That
takes willpower.

WAITING FOREVER

When you quit with the willpower method you are constantly waiting for the moment when you know you are free. It's a moment that never comes.

With Easyway there is nothing to wait for. You are free the moment you unravel all the illusions that have led you into the debt trap, free yourself from fear and stop incurring new debts.

The feeling of elation and excitement is immediate.

CROSSING THE LINE
THE EASY WAY

Curing your debt problem is easy with
this method. Follow all the instructions
and you can't fail to cross the line. But
you'll only get to that line if you're in a
positive frame of mind. If you continue
to believe that you have to suffer an
indeterminate period of misery, you'll
feel fearful, deprived and miserable.
You will again seek to relieve those
feelings by overspending and you'll fall
back into the trap.

YOU DON'T NEED WILLPOWER

People who try to stop through willpower do experience a boost when they give in and go on a spending spree. This is not a genuine pleasure but a temporary relief from the self-inflicted suffering of the willpower method. It is quickly followed by feelings of failure, guilt and disappointment.

You only suffer a feeling of deprivation if you continue to believe that spending gives you a genuine pleasure or crutch.

You only need willpower if you have a conflict of will, a tug-of-war in your mind. Take away one side of the tug-of-war and there is nothing to pull against. It's easy.

THE ADDICTIVE PERSONALITY

Many debtors are also heavy drinkers or smokers. These multiple addictions lead a lot of so-called experts to believe there is something in their genetic make-up that makes them predisposed to being an addict – an addictive personality.

Addicts are only too happy to go along with this theory because it gives them the perfect excuse: 'I would quit but I simply can't – it's the way I'm made!'

If you believe you have an addictive personality, you are consigning yourself to life in the trap.

WHY SOME ADDICTS ARE MORE TRAPPED THAN OTHERS

Why can one person restrict herself to the occasional spree, while another ends up junk spending every day and blowing every penny?

The simple answer is that we are all different and the void is different for all of us. The lengths we go to in our efforts to fill it vary, as do the circumstances in which we live. Time and opportunity will play a part in how much debt we are able to incur.

There are countless factors that influence how quickly we descend into the trap, but an addictive personality is not one of them.

AN AFFINITY OF WEAKNESSES

The various character traits that problem debtors share – unstable temperament, a tendency towards excess, high susceptibility to stress, evasiveness, anxiety, insecurity – are caused by debt.

The reason they feel more comfortable in each other's company is not because their fellow addicts are more interesting or fun; on the contrary, it's because they won't challenge each other or make each other think twice about their addiction because they're in the same boat.

All addicts know they are slavishly doing something stupid and self-destructive. They don't like to be reminded of the fact.

THE EVIDENCE OF HISTORY

If there was a gene that predisposed
people to become addicts, you would
expect the percentage of addicts in the
world to have remained fairly constant
throughout recorded history. But gambling
addiction, for example, is rapidly on the
rise throughout the world. Smoking, on the
other hand, is falling in the West but rising
in Asia. What complex genetic anomaly is
this that rises and falls so rapidly, and even
appears to transfer itself wholesale from
one continent to another?

THE EFFECT NOT THE CAUSE

You didn't become addicted to spending because you have an addictive personality. If you think you have an addictive personality, it's simply because you became addicted to spending. I've explained how addiction takes hold. Before you got hooked, you had no need or desire to overspend.

This is the trick that addiction plays on you. It makes you think that you're dependent on your addiction and that there's some weakness in your character or genetic make-up. It maintains its grip on you by distorting your perceptions.

WHY WE CONTINUE TO OVERSPEND

We first start spending beyond our means because we have been brainwashed into believing that it will give us some form of pleasure or a crutch. The reason we continue to do it is that we are chasing an impossible goal.

I call that goal fulfilment – the sense that everything has been restored and you can walk away happy. Spending addicts never feel fulfilled, but instead of seeing that overspending is causing the unfulfilled feeling, they assume they have to spend more.

While you go on incurring new debts, you can never feel fulfilled.

ESSENTIAL DEBT

You probably believe that a certain amount of debt is unavoidable. After all, is it not the case that in order to make your way in a civilized society you have to acquire certain properties or services, which, unless you are lucky enough to have vast personal wealth, can only be acquired by incurring some degree of debt? A car loan, a mortgage or a student loan, for example.

The obvious answer is yes. The actual answer is no.

Think about it: nobody has to own a car, nobody has to go to college and nobody has to own a house.

NEED V. WANT

Don't worry, I'm not about to tell you that you need to go and live in a shack and fetch your water from a stream – though some people do choose such a way of life and are very happy with it. I am merely stating that none of these things are essential to our survival on this planet. They are all choices we make in the belief that they will enhance our quality of life.

Apart from food, it's rare that we buy anything because we really need it. Not want it, need it. Want is the desire to fill an emotional void. Need is fundamental to survival.

BE GOOD TO YOURSELF

Neither am I telling you that you don't need to buy new shoes because the old ones aren't killing you yet. Wearing old shoes can be a miserable experience. Our aim is to stop you feeling miserable. So if your old shoes are making you miserable, I would argue that you do need a new pair.

The distinction between want and need varies from person to person, because need includes the need for happiness. The important thing is to be honest with yourself.

Stop to think about want and need every time you spend and you will quickly become adept at identifying the purchases you don't need.

WILLIAM MORRIS

Try applying the golden rule put forward by William Morris, the 19th century English artist and writer, most famous for his beautiful textile designs:

'Have nothing in your house that you do not know to be useful, or believe to be beautiful.'

Look around your home and apply this rule to everything you see. Be very honest. You will begin to see the true value in things: some will seem more precious than you thought; others will reveal themselves as worthless.

Morris's philosophy is a good way of distinguishing between want and need.

CHOOSE TO ESCAPE

Our parents and other influences encourage us to spend in order to make ourselves happy, and in believing that spending is the route to happiness we lose control.

You have a choice about everything you buy, but until you understand that you have a choice you won't be able to exercise it. Addicts believe they have no choice. That is because they feel trapped. Once you accept that you do have a choice, escape from the trap becomes easy.

THE FOURTH INSTRUCTION

The truth is that nobody genuinely enjoys junk spending – they only think they do because they've been fed a constant stream of misinformation that creates a want. The small buzz you get from spending reduces that want momentarily, but then leaves you feeling more empty than before. You mistake the emptiness for a need to spend and so you repeat the process. That's how you get hooked.

It's essential that you stop kidding yourself that junk spending gives you pleasure.

Fourth instruction: DISREGARD ALL ATTEMPTS TO SELL YOU THINGS YOU DON'T NEED.

EXCUSES

Like all addicts, overspenders are always making excuses.

'You've got to live a little.'
'I deserve it.'
'Money talks.'
'No one likes a miser.'
'I'm not good with money.'

They kid themselves that there's something special about their situation that makes debt inevitable. But they are all caught in the same trap because they all believe the same thing: that spending money is a source of pleasure or a crutch.

SELF-ESTEEM

Most people with debt problems suffer from low self-esteem. That's not because people with low self-esteem are more prone to get into debt, but because having debt problems causes low self-esteem. The longer you remain in debt, the more miserable it's going to get.

When you start to reverse your descent into debt, you'll find that your self-image changes very quickly and you'll enjoy a renewed sense of self-worth.

WAITING FOR A WINDFALL

If you're waiting for a windfall to clear your debts, I'm afraid you're deluding yourself. You're considerably more likely to be struck by lightning than to win the lottery.

Even if you were to receive a surprise windfall, it wouldn't solve your problem. Unless the brainwashing that has led you to overspend is removed, you would go and spend larger amounts and it would only be a matter of time before your money worries returned.

WHEN MONEY BECOMES GOD

Please get this straight: whether you are careful with money or reckless with it, money itself will not make you happy. In order to understand the true purpose and value of money, you have to strip away the brainwashing.

We've been fooled into believing that money is the key to happiness, but it is merely a means by which to acquire things. Those things should be a source of happiness and pleasure, but the money with which you buy them is nothing more than a tool, like the wrench that tightens the nut that enables a child to ride his bicycle.

THE TREADMILL

It's time for you now to step off the treadmill and escape the vicious circle. I use the term 'step off' because it really is as easy as that. You merely need to keep an open mind.

The treadmill is the fruitless pursuit of happiness through spending money. As I've explained, the more you try to find fulfilment through spending, the more unfulfilled you feel. The only way to stop this trend is to step off the treadmill altogether. Open your mind and come with me on an exciting journey.

THE ESSENTIALS FOR HAPPINESS

In order to survive on this planet, there are only three things you need: food, warmth and shelter. If you think that's not enough to make you happy, may I remind you to keep an open mind?

Let me tell you about one of my happiest memories from childhood. I'm sitting alone on a rock by the sea, fishing. The sun is shining brightly and I'm in my swimming trunks. That's all I have: a fishing rod and a pair of swimming trunks and I'm as happy as can be.

THE FIFTH INSTRUCTION

You are about to stop your descent into the debt trap once and for all. From now on, whenever you find yourself in a situation where you're tempted to buy something, I want you to follow my next instruction.

Fifth instruction: IF YOU CAN'T AFFORD IT, LEAVE IT.

Don't worry about your existing debts for now – we will take care of those in due course. The most important thing is that you stop incurring more debt NOW. You have a simple choice: choose to follow my instructions and become debt-free or choose to continue your life of debt misery by spending money you don't have.

THE BEST THINGS IN LIFE ARE FREE

Doesn't it strike you as strange that as we become adults and acquire the means to 'treat' ourselves to more and more indulgences, we find it harder and harder to achieve the level of untainted happiness that we enjoyed as children, and that moments such as my fishing experience become increasingly rare?

What is it you crave when you need to get away from it all? Sunshine? Water? Grass? Trees? Mountains? Peace and quiet? Can you tell me what any of those things actually cost?

THE FIRST ESSENTIAL

Once you accept that there are only three essentials for survival, it's easy to accept that everything else is a matter of personal choice.

You don't need me to tell you that food and water are essential. Yet one of the biggest health problems facing the world today is obesity. This problem is evidence that we have become confused about our need for food and water in a similar way to how we've become confused about our need to spend money. It's not simply an issue of consuming too much, it's also an issue of consuming the wrong things.

HEALTHY EATING: CAN YOU AFFORD IT?

If you want to save money on food and eat well, remember that the best way to satisfy hunger is to eat nutritious food. Fresh fruit, vegetables, nuts and grains will give you all the nutrients you need in the quickest time. They also happen to be the foods that naturally taste best.

Eating healthy food actually saves money:

1. It costs less to buy.

2. You don't have to supplement it with more food to satisfy your hunger, or the false hunger created by the addiction to refined sugar.

3. It keeps you healthy and energetic, meaning less time off work and less money spent on medical treatment.

THE SECOND ESSENTIAL

We spend a lot of money on keeping warm
but there are a number of things you can
do to reduce your fuel costs.

Get free advice and financial help with
insulating your property.

Restrict the heating and lighting to only
the rooms you're using.

Scan the market for the cheapest tariffs and
press your supplier for the best deal you
can get.

Wear more clothes around the home.

FASHION SLAVERY

Clothes aren't just for keeping warm. It's important to dress in a way that makes you feel good about yourself, but being a slave to fashion will not lead to fulfilment. The fashion industry is very clever and very manipulative. It is constantly changing its messages, inventing new rules about beauty and style and preying on our deepest insecurities in order to make us keep buying more and more junk that we don't need. We can never quite catch up, so why even try?

Step off the treadmill!

THE THIRD ESSENTIAL

For most of us, the need for shelter results in the biggest single expense of all: a roof over our heads. The property market is built on a staggering level of debt. People who never dream of letting their bank account go into the red think nothing of borrowing hundreds of thousands of pounds to buy a house.

Sign up to a lifestyle you can't afford and you run the risk of losing your home. Or, in other words, being deprived of the third essential.

MY HOUSE, MY CASTLE

We have come to expect to live in properties that are far bigger than we need. It's a common delusion: that the size of your home says something about who you are. Kings and queens live in palaces; paupers live in shacks. But the belief that a big house amounts to a successful life is as false as the belief that expensive cars or a big wardrobe will bring you happiness.

There's nothing wrong with living in a big house if it makes you happy. But the financial pressure we put ourselves under to afford the extra space often negates any pleasure.

Don't confuse excess with success!

THE CREDIT PROPOSITION

Say you'd never heard of credit cards and I tried to sell you the idea: 'Here, try this piece of plastic. It fits neatly inside your wallet and whenever you want to buy something, all you have to do is hand it to the shopkeeper and thereby ensure that you pay more than the advertised price.'

It's a ludicrous proposition, especially for someone with debt problems. So why are so many people, even those already in debt, seduced by credit cards to the point where they believe they can't live without them?

THE CONVENIENCE DELUSION

A supposed advantage of credit cards is that they remove the obstacles that prevent you from buying. One obstacle is not having enough money; another is the thought process you would go through in weighing up how you want to spend your money.

Both of these 'obstacles' are actually essential considerations in keeping out of debt. They are considerations that people who are not in debt apply all the time and they are considerations you applied quite comfortably before you fell into the credit trap.

The longer you go on using a credit card, the less affordable everything becomes. Credit card debt makes everything more expensive.

THE RESPECT DELUSION

People think their credit card earns them respect. The process you go through in applying for a card is designed to make you think you've been carefully chosen. And by giving you the honour of qualifying for a gold card, the credit companies make you feel like you've been welcomed into some privileged club.

But they don't respect you, they're laughing at you. Every time you 'flash the card', they're laughing all the way to the bank.

THE CONTROL DELUSION

Everyone who signs up for a credit card begins with the same intentions. 'I'll pay off the balance each month, no problem.' The card actually appears to give them more control over their money. But the reality is that our best intentions are easily abandoned, especially when times get hard or we need cheering up.

Credit cards do not give you control – they are designed to lure you into the debt trap.

THE NEED DELUSION

It's a common misconception that if you're renting a car or hiring a piece of equipment you have to have a credit card to offer as collateral, and for identification. This is not so. Most hire firms offer alternatives. It may involve making arrangements in advance, taking ID and paying the deposit by debit card or in cash, but it can be done and it's really not that inconvenient.

THE CASH FLOW DELUSION

Claiming that your credit card helps your cash flow is really just a way of saying, 'It allows me to buy things I can't afford.' This is only going to result in one more debt.

If you have the regular income to pay off your balance every month, then you don't need to go into debt in the first place. All you have to do is shift the cycle so that your bumper periods precede your lean ones, rather than the other way around.

INTO THE BLACK

Everything costs more when you keep your finances in the red, because you have to pay interest on top of the purchase price of everything you buy.

Some people feel restricted by staying in the black, but there is a limit when you're in the red too: your credit limit.

Take two people on the same income leading exactly the same life: person A who keeps his finances in the black, person B who stays in the red. Over time, person A will become richer while person B gets poorer.

Who is making the sensible choice?

FIRST STEPS OUT OF DEBT

If you have followed all the instructions so far, you have come a long way towards achieving the state of mind necessary for you to quit incurring new debts and to turn the tide, so that you can get out of the red and into the black.

You have every reason to feel excited. Though it may feel like a deep, dark hole, there's no physical effort required to escape the debt trap. You simply need to make a choice. It's a simple choice between taking a step backward or a step forward.

DON'T BANK ON BANKRUPTCY

You will no doubt have heard of people who fell heavily into debt but were able to declare themselves bankrupt and have all their debts wiped out by the courts. Perhaps you think this is your ideal solution.

Forget it!

More than half the people who go bankrupt will do so again. Bankruptcy solves nothing for them because it does not tackle the real problem: their addiction to overspending. As soon as they are legally permitted, they start running up debts again – not to mention alienating friends and family from whom they continue to borrow without repaying.

TIME TO TAKE CONTROL

If you still have doubts and fears, don't worry, that's perfectly normal. You've been brainwashed into thinking you have to make huge sacrifices to get out of debt; that the process will be hard and miserable; and that, even if you do succeed, you will be forever tempted to get back into debt again. If you have kept an open mind, you will realize by now that the fears you had about getting out of debt were mere illusions brought about by brainwashing, and so they were not genuine fears at all.

Remind yourself that you have nothing to fear and prepare to take that first forward step.

NO 'GET OUT' CLAUSE

Some addicts, once they realize that fear is the only thing preventing them from quitting, try to allay their fear by telling themselves they can always relapse if it gets too hard. In other words, quitting doesn't have to be final. Start with that attitude and you will almost certainly fail. With this method, quitting is final because you have no need or desire to relapse. Start with the certainty that you are going to find it easy to succeed.

IMPORTANT REMINDERS

Remember these three very important facts as we move forward:

1. **Junk spending does absolutely nothing for you at all.**

2. **There is no need for a transitional period before getting absolutely free.**

3. **There is no such thing as 'just this once' or 'the occasional spree'.**

WILL IT MAKE ME A MISER?

On the contrary. Misers are miserable and my objective is to help you free yourself from misery.

Generosity is a great source of happiness. Once you've quit junk spending, you will find that you have more money to spend not only on yourself but also on others and you will gain much more from the money you do spend.

And remember, junk spending does absolutely nothing for you. It is not a source of happiness. You don't have to spend money to be happy. The best things in life really are free.

NAME YOUR PLEASURES

Take a pen and paper and write down
all the activities that give you genuine
pleasure. Really think about it. Take a day
or two over it if you like and write down
the things you enjoy as they come to mind.
Focus on the times when you feel most
relaxed and happy, and when your debts
are furthest from your mind. This will help
you to become aware of what you really
enjoy and value in life.

REJOICE IN VICTORY

When you rid yourself of a mortal enemy, there is no need to mourn. On the contrary, you can rejoice and celebrate from the start, and you can continue to rejoice and celebrate for the rest of your life.

Get it clear in your mind that junk spending is not your friend, nor is it part of your identity. It never has been. It's your mortal enemy and by getting rid of it you're sacrificing nothing, just making marvellous, positive gains.

THINK ABOUT IT

Or rather, don't try not to think about junk spending.

Forcing your mind to close on a subject is not the way to tackle it. Unlike people who quit with the willpower method, you'll be happy to think about your old enemy and you needn't try to block it from your mind. Trying not to think about something is a sure way of becoming obsessed with it. If I tell you not to think about elephants, what's the first thing that comes into your head?

Exactly!

THE TURNING POINT

We are at the turning point in your debt problem, the point at which you begin to reverse the flow of your finances.

Imagine you're walking along a path through a forest. All the time you have been increasing your debts you have been walking in the wrong direction and the forest has been growing denser and denser all around you. All you need to do is turn around and start walking in the opposite direction.

But first you need to stop walking deeper into the forest. In other words, you need to stop taking on new debts.

THE SIXTH INSTRUCTION

The moment you stop borrowing is the turning point. And the first thing you can do to stop borrowing is to destroy the plastic that makes it so easy and mindless.

Sixth instruction: DESTROY ALL YOUR CREDIT CARDS AND STORE CARDS AND REMOVE ANY OTHER SOURCES OF DEBT.

Get it clear in your mind: nothing bad is happening, you are not making a sacrifice and there is no reason to feel deprived. Cut through that plastic with relish and enjoy dumping the source of so much misery in the rubbish bin for good.

THE SEVENTH INSTRUCTION

If you're wondering when would be the best time to follow that last instruction, all you need to do is follow the seventh instruction. Perhaps you think it's best to wait until after the weekend, or maybe there's an event coming up, such as a birthday or Christmas, which you should get out of the way before you make your move.

The seventh instruction: DO IT NOW!

There is nothing to gain by waiting. The moment you stop incurring new debts is the moment you become free.

REMOVE ALL DOUBT

Make a solemn vow that you will never overspend again.

With other important decisions in life, we can never be sure they're correct. Even if we don't regret them years later, we can never know what would have happened if we had done something else. The beauty about the vow you are about to make is that you know it's the correct decision, even as you make it.

Having made your vow, never even begin to question or doubt that decision.

WELCOME TO FREEDOM!

You don't have to wait until you've cleared all your debts before rejoicing in the knowledge that you're free from the debt trap. Once you know you have a solution to a problem, you no longer need to worry about it. It might take some time for the problem to be fully resolved, but you overcome it the moment you find the solution.

The solution to your debt problem is not incurring new debt. Now that you know and understand that you have no need or desire to spend money you don't have, you can start enjoying your freedom immediately.

Congratulations! You're free!

DEBT VS. DEBT PROBLEM

Perhaps you think you still have a huge way to go before you can say you no longer have a debt problem. Not so. You still have debts, but you no longer have a problem. You can begin the process of getting out of the red at once.

Start by keeping an accurate record of your spending. Make a note of every penny you spend and collate your records in a monthly spending sheet, arranged in categories such as 'transport', 'groceries', etc. Include your regular outgoings, e.g. domestic fuel bills, telephone, water, etc.

Keep essentials and non-essentials separate. For example, apples and chocolate should not be lumped together under 'food'.

CALCULATE YOUR DEFICIT

Add up all the outgoings on your monthly spending log. Now write down your total income for the month, after deductions for tax, etc. Make sure you include every source of income that you have. If your monthly income varies, take an average for the last 12 months.

Now subtract your income from your outgoings. What you're left with is the amount by which you lose money each month, so write a 'minus' sign in front of this figure. Our aim is to turn that minus into a plus.

YOUR ROUTE MAP OUT OF DEBT

Create a new sheet with 'Category' and 'Spend' columns like the monthly spending log, and add two more columns headed 'Plan' and '+/-'. This will be your route map out of debt.

Copy across all categories that qualify as essentials: Food, Warmth or Shelter. Also include your repayments on loans, as you have no choice over these payments. Copy the amounts from the spending log into the 'Plan' column. The 'Spend' column will be used to record next month's outgoings.

Leave a one-line space, draw a line under the essentials and now copy across all your other outgoings, in order of priority. How you prioritize them is entirely up to you.

FOCUS ON THE ESSENTIALS

Add up your total spend on essentials and deduct it from your monthly income. If you are left with a minus figure, something has to change. Either you need to earn more money or you need to find a way to reduce your essential outgoings, such as cutting your heating bills or finding somewhere cheaper to live.

It may mean taking a difficult decision, but you cannot get out of debt if your spending on essentials is greater than your income.

WEIGH UP THE NON-ESSENTIALS

If your income is greater than the sum of your essential outgoings, the difference is the amount you have left to spend on non-essentials. Write this figure down separately.

Now add up the figures you wrote in your 'plan' column for non-essentials and deduct it from the figure you just wrote down. If you get a minus figure, then you need to reduce your planned spending on non-essentials.

BALANCE THE BOOKS

You now need to reduce your planned spending on non-essentials until the books balance with at least £1 to spare.

Be brutally honest about the things you think you need or want. Remember William Morris. Keep an open mind and be imaginative about ways to reduce your spending. Could you walk to work, or at least get off a stop earlier? Eat more healthily and cut out the snacks? Buy fewer clothes but nicer ones?

Remember, everything below the essentials line is non-essential.

THE FOURTH ESSENTIAL

In the blank space you left above the line you drew under essentials in the category column, I now want you to write 'Debt Repayment'. Remember, this plan is your route map out of debt. It's time to start clearing those debts.

Eighth instruction: MAKE DEBT REPAYMENT YOUR FOURTH ESSENTIAL.

To begin with, just £1 in the 'Plan' column will do. But unlike the figures below the line, it's not negotiable. Whatever you write down in your plan for 'Debt Repayment', you must pay it.

PAYING OFF THE CAPITAL

Make a list of everyone to whom you owe money and how much. There's no need to include your mortgage, if you have one, because that's already accounted for in your financial plan. However, if you've fallen behind with your repayments, or your rent, you need to include that amount in your debt list.

Add them all up and calculate each individual debt as a percentage of the total. Now divide the amount you have made available for Debt Repayment among all your creditors according to these percentages.

Example:
Creditor A = 50%
Debt Repayment = £20
Repayment to Creditor A = £10

ROBBING PETER TO PAY PAUL

It's not uncommon for people with money worries to have funds tucked away in a savings or investment account. Despite the pressure they're suffering from their mounting debts, they refuse to touch this money. They have ring-fenced it for retirement or 'a rainy day' and they regard it as something sacred.

Out of fear of being destitute in their old age, or perhaps at some point before that, they are ensuring that they are suffering the misery of being destitute NOW!

It's almost guaranteed that any interest on savings won't be as much as you're being charged on your debts, so use any savings to reduce your debts.

FROM SMALL ACORNS

You're probably thinking, 'At £20 a month, I'm never going to pay off my £28,500 debt.' But the fact that you're repaying anything marks a major turnaround in the way you control your finances.

You are now in control.

When you start to pay off the capital, you automatically and immediately reduce your outgoings as your interest payments are reduced. Use the money saved to increase your debt repayments, allocating it to the creditor that's charging you the highest interest rate until that debt is paid off.

You will soon see your rate of repayment begin to accelerate. Enjoy this journey from day one.

CONCLUSION

The main aim of this book is your happiness. I wanted to show you that if we see money as more than just a tool, we become its slave and that can cause misery. That's why I did not set out simply with the aim of getting you to clear your debts, but first to remove the illusions that create the desire to incur new debts.

If you have followed all the instructions, congratulations! You have achieved something marvellous. Not only have you taken practical steps to pay off your debts, you have done something you thought you could never do: you have put a stop to the slavery.

Now you can start enjoying life to the full. Your repayment plan will take care of itself now that you're taking care of yourself.

THE INSTRUCTIONS

1. FOLLOW ALL THE INSTRUCTIONS.

2. KEEP AN OPEN MIND.

3. START OFF IN A HAPPY FRAME OF MIND RATHER THAN WITH A FEELING OF DOOM AND GLOOM.

4. DISREGARD ALL ATTEMPTS TO SELL YOU THINGS YOU DON'T NEED.

5. IF YOU CAN'T AFFORD IT, LEAVE IT.

6. DESTROY ALL YOUR CREDIT CARDS AND STORE CARDS AND REMOVE ANY OTHER SOURCES OF DEBT.

7. DO IT NOW!

8. MAKE DEBT REPAYMENT YOUR FOURTH ESSENTIAL.

YIPPEE, I'M FREE!

TELL ALLEN CARR'S EASYWAY ORGANISATION THAT YOU'VE ESCAPED

Leave a comment on www.allencarr.com,
email yippee@allencarr.com, like our Facebook page
www.facebook.com/AllenCarr
or write to the Worldwide Head Office address
shown below.

ALLEN CARR'S EASYWAY CLINICS

The following list indicates the countries where
Allen Carr's Easyway To Stop Smoking Clinics are
currently operational. Check www.allencarr.com
for latest additions to this list. The success rate at
the clinics, based on the three month money-back
guarantee, is over 90 per cent.

Selected clinics also offer sessions that deal with
alcohol, other drugs, and weight issues. Please check
with your nearest clinic, listed below, for details.

Allen Carr's Easyway guarantees that you will find it
easy to stop at the clinics or your money back.

ALLEN CARR'S EASYWAY

Worldwide Head Office
Park House, 14 Pepys Road, Raynes Park,
London SW20 8NH ENGLAND
Tel: +44 (0)208 9447761
Email: mail@allencarr.com
Website: www.allencarr.com

Worldwide Press Office

Tel: +44 (0)7970 88 44 52

Email: jd@allencarr.com

UK Clinic Information and Central Booking

Line 0800 389 2115 (Freephone)

UNITED KINGDOM	JAPAN
REPUBLIC OF IRELAND	LATVIA
AUSTRALIA	LEBANON
AUSTRIA	LITHUANIA
BELGIUM	MAURITIUS
BRAZIL	MEXICO
BULGARIA	NETHERLANDS
CANADA	NEW ZEALAND
CHILE	NORWAY
COLOMBIA	PERU
CYPRUS	POLAND
DENMARK	PORTUGAL
ECUADOR	ROMANIA
ESTONIA	RUSSIA
FINLAND	SERBIA
FRANCE	SINGAPORE
GERMANY	SLOVENIA
GREECE	SOUTH AFRICA
GUATEMALA	SOUTH KOREA
HONG KONG	SPAIN
HUNGARY	SWEDEN
ICELAND	SWITZERLAND
INDIA	TURKEY
ISRAEL	UKRAINE
ITALY	USA

Visit www.allencarr.com to access your nearest clinic's contact details.

OTHER ALLEN CARR PUBLICATIONS

Allen Carr's revolutionary Easyway method is available in a wide variety of formats, including digitally as audiobooks and ebooks, and has been successfully applied to a broad range of subjects. For more information about Easyway publications, please visit
shop.allencarr.com

Good Sugar Bad Sugar

The Easy Way for Women to Lose Weight

The Easy Way to Quit Sugar

No More Diets

Stop Smoking with Allen Carr
(with 70-minute audio CD)

Stop Smoking Now
(with hypnotherapy CD)

Your Personal Stop Smoking Plan

The Easy Way to Stop Smoking

The Easy Way for

Women to Stop Smoking

Easyway Express: Stop Smoking and Quit E-cigarettes
(ebook)

The Only Way to Stop Smoking Permanently

The Illustrated Easy Way to Stop Smoking

The Illustrated Easy Way for Women to Stop Smoking

The Nicotine Conspiracy
(ebook)

How to Be a Happy

Nonsmoker
(ebook)

No More Ashtrays

Finally Free!

How to Stop Your Child Smoking

The Little Book of Quitting

Smoking Sucks (Parent Guide with 16 page pull-out comic) (ebook)

Stop Drinking Now (with hypnotherapy CD)

The Easy Way to Control Alcohol

Your Personal Stop Drinking Plan

The Illustrated Easy Way to Stop Drinking

The Easy Way for Women to Stop Drinking

No More Hangovers

Lose Weight Now (with hypnotherapy CD)

The Easy Way to Stop Gambling

No More Gambling (ebook)

Get Out of Debt Now

The Easy Way to Enjoy Flying

No More Fear of Flying

Burning Ambition

No More Worrying

Packing It In The Easy Way (the autobiography)